D1190185

Taking Toys Apart

By Kristin Fontichiaro

CHERRY LAKE Publishing

Published in the United States of America by
Cherry Lake Publishing
Ann Arbor, Michigan
www.cherrylakepublishing.com

Series Editor: Kristin Fontichiaro
Photo Credits: Cover and pages 6, 8, 10, 12, 14, 16, and 18,
Kristin Fontichiaro; pages 4 and 20 left: Michigan Makers/
Regents of the University of Michigan.

Library of Congress Cataloging-in-Publication Data has been filed and is available at
catalog.loc.gov

Cherry Lake Publishing would like to acknowledge the work of the Partnership for
21st Century Learning. Please visit *www.p21.org* for more information.

Printed in the United States of America
Corporate Graphics

A Note to Adults: Please review the instructions for the activities in this book before allowing children to do them. Be sure to help them with any activities you do not think they can safely complete on their own.

A Note to Kids: Be sure to ask an adult for help with these activities when you need it. Always put your safety first!

Table of Contents

When you look inside your toys, you can learn a lot about how things work.

What's Inside Your Toys?

Have you ever wondered what is inside your toys? What makes them move or make noise? How do they do what they do? To get started, you need a toy that has moving parts and batteries. You might find one at a **thrift store**. Or maybe you are ready to get rid of an old toy. Ask an adult before you take anything apart.

Stay Away from Screens

Do not pick a toy with a display screen, such as a portable video game. Those screens may contain dangerous chemicals.

Be sure to gather your tools before you start.

Tools

In addition to a toy, you will also need:

- Safety glasses or goggles to protect your eyes

- Needle-nose pliers to hold on to things extra tightly

- Safety gloves to protect your hands

- Scissors to cut wires or stuffed animal parts

- Screwdrivers to take out screws

- A bowl to put parts in

You'll likely need a variety of screwdrivers to get your toys apart.

Get to Know Your Screwdrivers

Most toy screws need a Phillips screwdriver. This kind of screwdriver has a plus-shaped tip. You will also need **precision** screwdrivers to take out very small screws inside your toy. Sometimes you need a screwdriver with a flat end to pry something apart.

Turning Screws

Remember the rule: "lefty loosey, righty tighty." It means turn the screwdriver left to unscrew. Turn it right to screw in a screw. When taking apart a toy, you will usually turn it left. Always press down lightly as you turn.

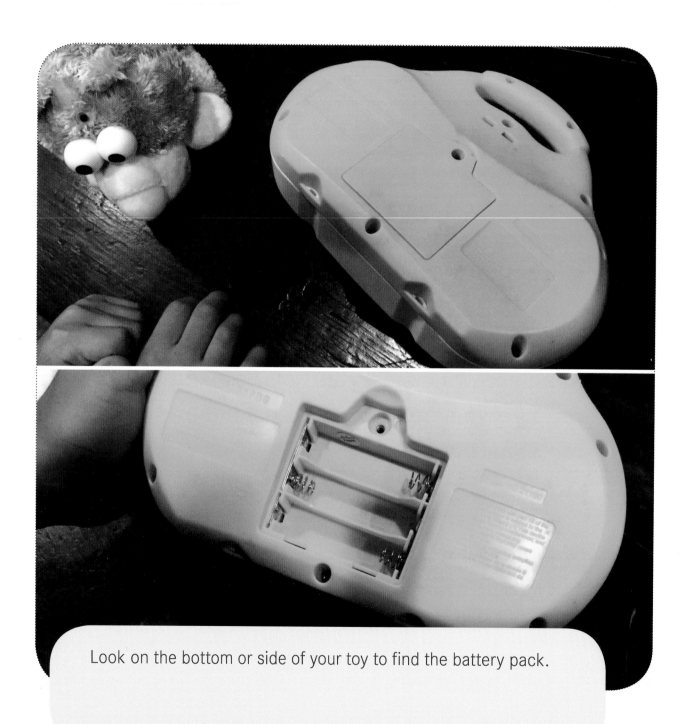

Look on the bottom or side of your toy to find the battery pack.

Power Down

Put on a pair of safety glasses or goggles. We need to make sure that no electricity is in your toy. Let's take out the batteries. Find the battery pack. It might have a cover with a picture of batteries on it. Sometimes the cover is screwed on. Take off the cover. Take out the batteries.

Can you see two wires coming out of the battery pack? Those connect the batteries to the toy's **circuit**. Energy moves from the battery, through the toy, and back to the battery in a circle.

Taking Off the Cover

Now look for the screws that are holding the toy's back cover on. Unscrew them. Gently open the cover. If it does not open, check that you have removed all of the screws. If it is still stuck, ask an adult to help you pry it open with a slotted screwdriver. Wear gloves to protect your fingers!

This circuit board has both solder and hot glue.

What's Inside: Circuit Boards

Every toy is made differently. However, most modern toys have small circuit boards inside. These are pieces of metal that have a circuit printed on them. They are usually green or blue. They act like the brain of your toy.

Solder and Hot Glue

Do you see little silver dots on the circuit board? They appear where metal parts connect to each other. Those silver dots are called **solder**. Solder is a kind of metal that melts to hold circuit parts together. Some toys use hot glue instead.

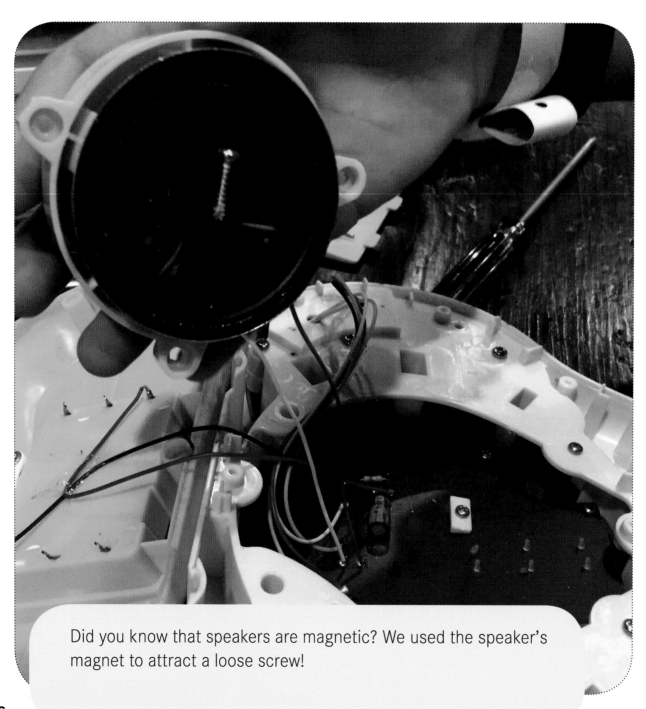

Did you know that speakers are magnetic? We used the speaker's magnet to attract a loose screw!

What's Inside: Speakers

Many toys make sounds or play music. That means your toy probably contains a speaker! You may have to unscrew a few more layers to find yours. Speakers are round. Some are silver, green, or black. If the speakers make the sound inside the toy, can you find the holes in the outer plastic where the sound comes out?

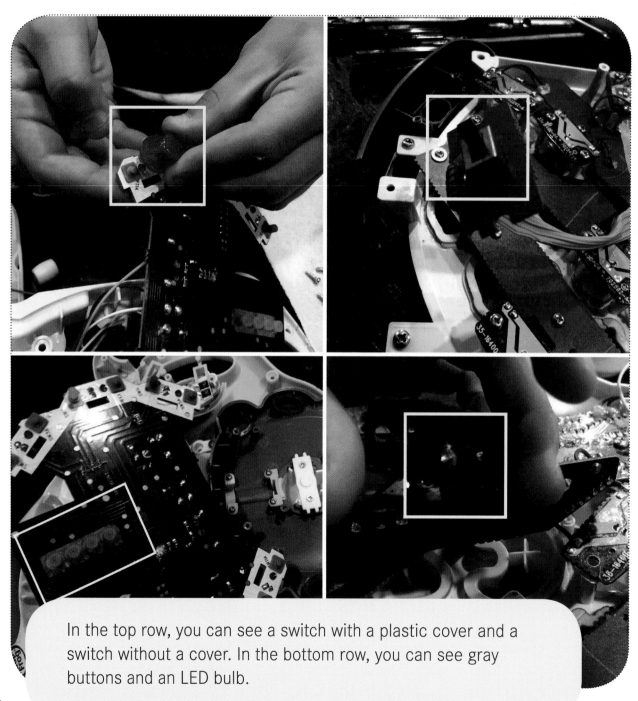

In the top row, you can see a switch with a plastic cover and a switch without a cover. In the bottom row, you can see gray buttons and an LED bulb.

What's Inside: Switches, Buttons, and Lights

If your toy has a switch, move it and see if anything happens on the inside.

Look for little rubber buttons. If you push a button on the outside of the toy, it will press the rubber button inside to complete a circuit and make something happen.

LEDs are tiny lightbulbs. If your toy lights up when you play with it, try to find the LEDs inside.

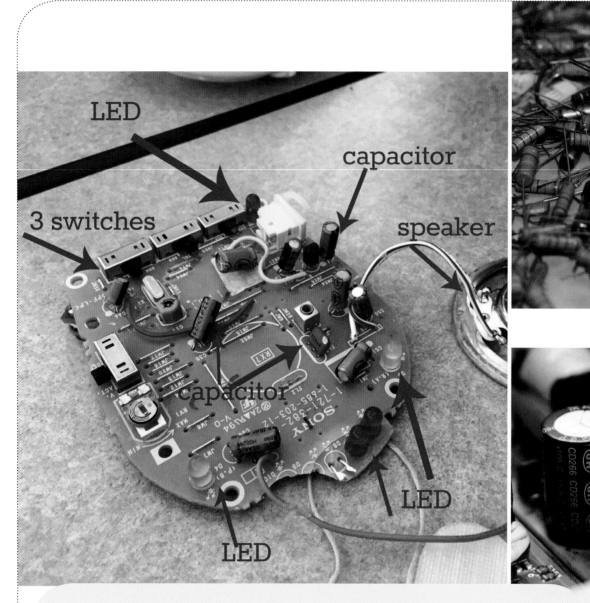

LED

capacitor

speaker

3 switches

capacitor

LED

LED

On the left is the circuit board of a baby monitor. On the top right is a pile of resistors. On the bottom right, you can see capacitors.

What's Inside: Capacitors and Resistors

Our toy tour ends with capacitors and resistors. You'll find them soldered onto circuit boards. Capacitors store energy inside your toy until it is needed. Sometimes they look like tiny cans or buttons. Don't open them up! Resistors absorb extra energy that your toy does not need. They look like tiny striped candies with a wire on each end.

Now you know the basics of what makes your toy work. What will you learn next?

Glossary

circuit (SUR-kit) a closed loop or path through which electricity can flow

LEDs (EL EE DEEZ) LED stands for "light-emitting diode"; an **LED** is a small bulb that lights up when electricity passes through it

precision (prih-SIZH-uhn) something done very carefully and accurately

solder (SAH-dur) a kind of metal that can be melted and used to attach other pieces of metal together

thrift store (THRIFT STOR) a store where people donate unwanted items so other people can buy them

Find Out More

Books

Lockwood, Sophie. *Super Cool Science Experiments: Electricity*.
Ann Arbor, MI: Cherry Lake Publishing, 2010.

Quinn, Amy. *Making Electric Jewelry*. Ann Arbor, MI: Cherry Lake
Publishing, 2017.

Web Sites

Exploratorium—The Tinkering Studio: Toy Take Apart
http://tinkering.exploratorium.edu/toy-take-apart
Check out some more ideas for taking toys apart and turning
them into new things.

Make Magazine—Quick Tip: Know Your Screwdrivers
*http://makezine.com/2016/10/31/quick-tip-know-your
-screwdrivers-hint-its-not-called-a-flathead*
Learn more about the different types of screwdrivers you can
use to take toys apart.

Index

About the Author

Kristin Fontichiaro makes and takes things apart at the University of Michigan School of Information. She thanks Quincy de Klerk, Grace de Klerk, and the Michigan Makers at Mitchell Elementary School for taking toys apart with her.